THE CYCLE OF PHOTOSYNTHESIS

by Arnold Ringstad

Published by The Child's World®
1980 Lookout Drive • Mankato, MN 56003-1705
800-599-READ • www.childsworld.com

Photographs ©: Juergen Faelchie/Shutterstock Images, cover (foreground), 1 (foreground); Shutterstock Images, cover (background), 1 (background), 10, 13, 20 (background), 20 (farmer); iStockphoto, 5, 9, 14, 17, 18; Natthapong Ponepormmarat/Shutterstock Images, 6

Copyright © 2019 by The Child's World®
All rights reserved. No part of the book may be reproduced or utilized in any form or by any means without written permission from the publisher.

ISBN 9781503828469
LCCN 2018944814

Printed in the United States of America
PA02396

About the Author

Arnold Ringstad has written more than 70 books for students. He especially enjoys reading and writing about space exploration. Ringstad lives in Minnesota with his wife and their cat.

Table of Contents

CHAPTER ONE
Making Life Possible ... 4

CHAPTER TWO
What Goes into the Cycle? ... 8

CHAPTER THREE
How Does Photosynthesis Work? ... 12

CHAPTER FOUR
The Results of Photosynthesis ... 16

Cycle of Photosynthesis Diagram ... 20

Fast Facts ... 21

Glossary ... 22

To Learn More ... 23

Index ... 24

CHAPTER ONE
Making Life Possible

Plants can be found nearly everywhere on Earth. Jungles are filled with dense trees and vines. Deserts have hardy cacti and bushes. In the ocean, seaweed and algae float along or live anchored to the seafloor. Grass and flowers grow in yards and parks. Earth's plants are often beautiful. They provide food for people and animals. They have another important role, too. They make life on Earth possible.

Animals need to breathe a **gas** called oxygen to survive. Plants create this oxygen. They do so in a process called photosynthesis.

The Amazon rain forest has thousands of tree types.

In photosynthesis, plants take in water and a gas called carbon dioxide. They also absorb energy from sunlight. This energy helps them turn the water and carbon dioxide into oxygen and sugar. Some oxygen goes into the **atmosphere**. The sugar is food for the plant. It can be used to help the plant grow. The plant can also store it to use later.

When animals breathe in oxygen, they breathe out carbon dioxide. Plants can then use the carbon dioxide to create more oxygen. This cycle makes it possible for plants and animals on Earth to survive.

Almost all plants need photosynthesis to grow and survive.

CHAPTER TWO
What Goes into the Cycle?

Photosynthesis requires a few important ingredients. Light, carbon dioxide, and water are all needed. All three things must be present for the process to happen.

The light for photosynthesis usually comes from the sun. The plant absorbs sunlight. This gives the plant the energy it needs for the process. The more light there is, the faster photosynthesis works.

The next ingredient is carbon dioxide. This gas is found in Earth's atmosphere. It is invisible to the eye. But it is an important part of photosynthesis. It enters plants through small holes in the leaves, stems, and other parts. These holes are called the **stomata**. When a plant gets more carbon dioxide, photosynthesis speeds up.

Gardeners need to be aware of how much sunlight certain plants should get.

Finally, plants need water. This comes from the environment around them. Falling rain and melting snow may deliver water to the plant. Some plants grow entirely underwater. Plants have structures that absorb water. In most plants, these structures are called roots.

To understand these ingredients, it is important to know about **atoms** and **molecules**. Atoms are very small particles. Molecules are groups of atoms that join together. Molecules make up specific substances, such as carbon dioxide and water.

Each carbon dioxide molecule is made up of one carbon atom and two oxygen atoms. Scientists call this CO_2. Each water molecule is made up of two hydrogen atoms and one oxygen atom. Hydrogen is a gas that doesn't have a color or smell. Scientists call water molecules H_2O. During photosynthesis, these molecules are split up. Then the atoms combine to form different substances.

Crocus flowers grow when snow hasn't fully melted yet.

CHAPTER THREE
How Does Photosynthesis Work?

Every living thing is made up of tiny parts called cells. Photosynthesis happens inside the cells of plants. Within plants' cells are structures called **chloroplasts**. The chloroplasts contain a green substance called chlorophyll. Chlorophyll is what absorbs energy from sunlight. It also gives most plants their green color.

Inside each chloroplast is a part called the thylakoid membrane. It looks like piles of flat discs. The space around these discs is called the stroma. Different parts of photosynthesis happen in the thylakoid membrane and in the stroma.

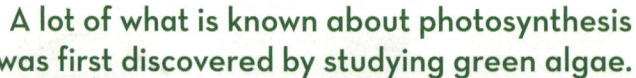
A lot of what is known about photosynthesis was first discovered by studying green algae.

In the thylakoid membrane, the energy from sunlight powers a **chemical reaction**. Water molecules are split apart into oxygen and hydrogen atoms. The oxygen leaves the plant as a gas. It exits through the stomata and enters the atmosphere.

The next part happens in the stroma. In the stroma, carbon dioxide molecules are split into carbon and oxygen atoms. The hydrogen atoms from the previous step join these atoms. They form a new molecule. It is a type of sugar called glucose. Each glucose molecule has six carbon atoms, 12 hydrogen atoms, and six oxygen atoms. Scientists call this $C_6H_{12}O_6$.

A person who is exercising breathes out more CO_2 than someone who is resting.

CHAPTER FOUR
The Results of Photosynthesis

Photosynthesis has two key products: oxygen and glucose. The oxygen that plants create is important to life on Earth. Without it, animals could not breathe. And without animals creating carbon dioxide, plants could not survive. Plants and animals cycle these gases through Earth's atmosphere.

Plants use glucose in two ways. First, they can use it as food. This makes them **autotrophs**. This means they make their own food. They use this food to grow. Second, plants can store glucose for later. The molecules are stored within their cells.

People are part of the cycle of photosynthesis.

Photosynthesis in the Sea

The kinds of plants people see every day, such as trees and grasses, make much of Earth's oxygen. However, a huge amount of oxygen is made in the sea. Tiny creatures called plankton and bacteria carry out photosynthesis there. Scientists believe they create one-third to one-half of the planet's oxygen.

When people eat plants, they get energy from this stored glucose. That glucose was made by photosynthesis. That means that energy from plants is originally energy from the sun.

In fact, all the food people eat is made possible by the sun. People eat animals such as chickens, cows, and fish. These creatures eat plants to get their energy. Some of that energy is stored in their bodies. And then people eat these animals to get that energy.

Photosynthesis is the key to life on Earth. It creates the air people breathe and the food people eat. It is one of the most important cycles in nature.

People use plants to make salads.

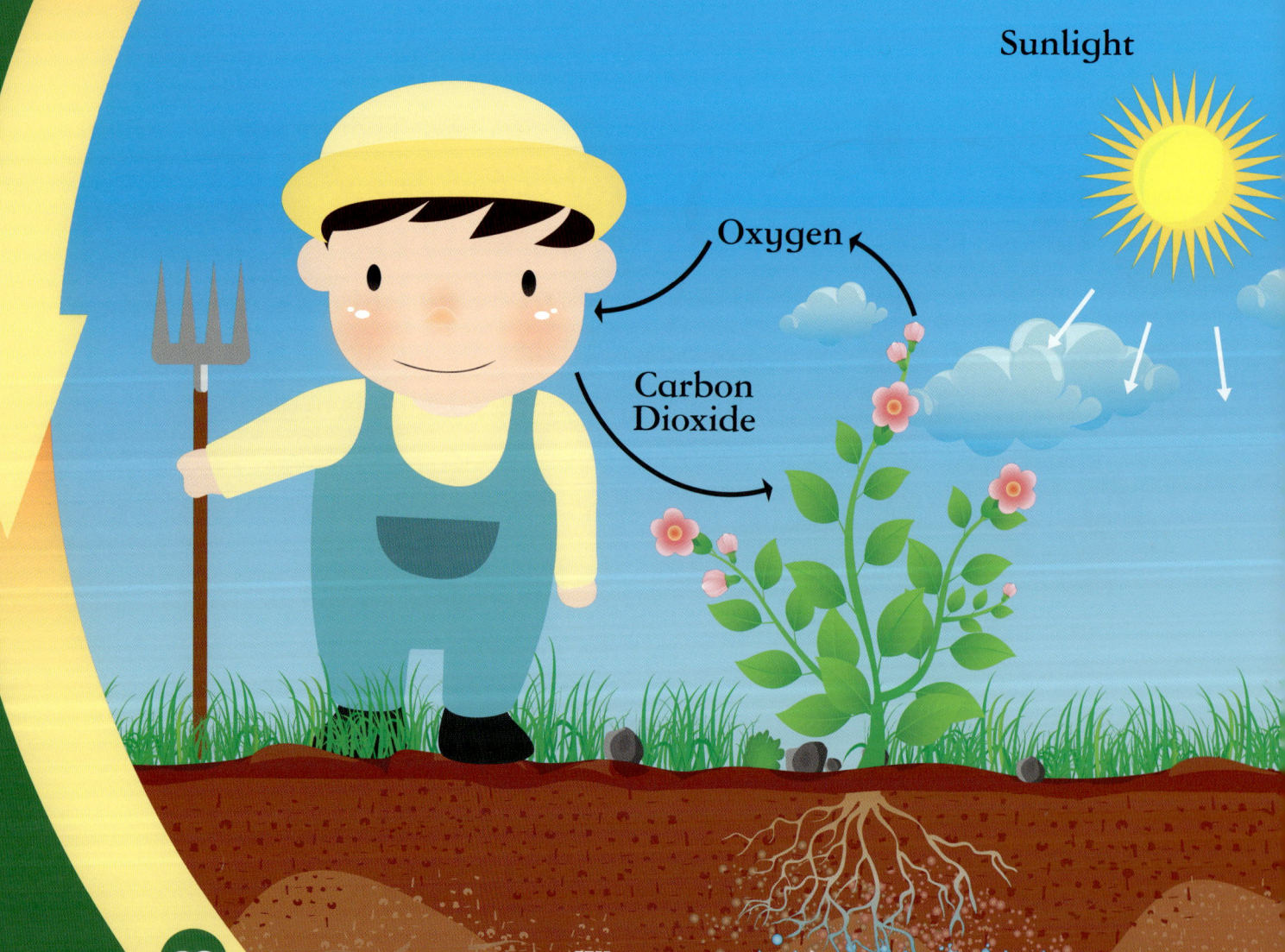

Fast Facts

- Plants carry out the process of photosynthesis.

- In photosynthesis, plants take in carbon dioxide and water. They also absorb energy from sunlight. Plants get carbon dioxide from people and animals.

- Photosynthesis takes place inside parts of plants' cells called chloroplasts.

- In the first part of photosynthesis, water molecules are split into hydrogen and oxygen atoms.

- In the second part of photosynthesis, carbon dioxide is split into carbon and oxygen atoms. Then, carbon, hydrogen, and oxygen combine to form glucose.

- Plants give off oxygen gas into the atmosphere. People and animals use this oxygen to breathe.

- Plants can use glucose to grow or store it for later use.

- The air people breathe and the food people eat is a product of the cycle of photosynthesis.

Glossary

atmosphere (AT-muhs-feer) The atmosphere is the gases surrounding Earth. Oxygen is in Earth's atmosphere.

atoms (AT-uhmz) Atoms are the basic building blocks of all matter. Oxygen, carbon, and hydrogen are examples of atoms.

autotrophs (AW-toh-trofs) Autotrophs are living things that make their own food. Plants are autotrophs.

chemical reaction (KEM-i-kuhl ree-AK-shun) A chemical reaction is a change that happens when materials combine and form a new material. A chemical reaction happens as a part of photosynthesis.

chloroplasts (KLOR-uh-plasts) Chloroplasts are the parts inside plant cells where photosynthesis takes place. Chloroplasts are needed for photosynthesis.

gas (GASS) Gas is a substance that usually floats through the air and expands to fill the space it is in. Carbon dioxide is a gas.

molecules (MAH-luh-kyoolz) Molecules are groups of atoms that join together and have special properties. Water and carbon dioxide are examples of molecules.

stomata (STOW-muh-tuh) Stomata are small holes on a plant's surface where gases can enter and leave the plant. Stomata are important to the photosynthesis process.

To Learn More

IN THE LIBRARY

Davis, Barbara J. *How Do Plants Get Food?* New York, NY: Chelsea Clubhouse, 2010.

Glaser, Chaya. *The Sun: A Super Star*. New York, NY: Bearport Publishing, 2015.

Lundgren, Julie K. *Plants Make Their Own Food*. Vero Beach, FL: Rourke Pub., 2012.

ON THE WEB

Visit our Web site for links about the cycle of photosynthesis:
childsworld.com/links

Note to Parents, Teachers, and Librarians: We routinely verify our Web links to make sure they are safe and active sites. So encourage your readers to check them out!

Index

atmosphere, 7, 8, 15, 16
atoms, 11, 15
autotrophs, 16

bacteria, 18

carbon dioxide, 7, 8, 11, 15, 16
chloroplasts, 12

energy, 7, 8, 12, 15, 19

glucose, 15, 16, 19

molecules, 11, 15, 16

plankton, 18

roots, 11

stomata, 8, 15
stroma, 12, 15

thylakoid membrane, 12, 15

Edison Twp. Free Public Library
340 Plainfield Ave.
Edison, New Jersey 08817

AUG 1 2 2019